I DID IT...

You Can, Too!

By

Fiona Harewood

Hope Publishers

4028 Castor Avenue
Philadelphia, PA 19124

The information in this booklet is meant to be inspirational. At the time of publication all links and web addresses referenced were working.

Copyright © 2011 by Hope Publishers

Publisher's Cataloging-In-Publication Data
(Prepared by The Donohue Group, Inc.)

Names: Harewood, Fiona, author.
Title: I did it ... you can, too! / by Fiona Harewood.
Description: First edition. | Philadelphia, PA : Hope Publishers, 2012. |
    Includes list of recommendations for further reading.
Identifiers: ISBN 9780983877400 (paperback) | ISBN 9780983877424
    (ebook)
Subjects: LCSH: Harewood, Fiona--Knowledge and learning. | Adult
    college students--Guidebooks. | Adult learning--Guidebooks. |
    Education, Higher. | Academic achievement. | Student aspirations. |
    Study skills.
Classification: LCC LC5215 .H285 2012 (print) | LCC LC5215 (ebook) |
    DDC 374--dc23

All rights reserved, including the right of reproduction in whole or in part in any form.

Printed in the United States of America First Edition:

February 2012

ISBN 978-0-9838774-0-0

cover design by We Read Literary Services
www.wereadliteraryservices.com

   visit "I Did It . . . You Can, Too!" on the web
         www.fionaharewood.com

> *"Give instruction to a wise man, and he will be yet wiser: teach a just man, and he will increase in learning."*
>
> *Proverbs 9:9*

ACKNOWLEDGEMENTS

All thanks and praises are due to my Heavenly Father, without whom, I can do nothing.

My heartfelt appreciation, love and gratitude to my husband, *Grantley*, for his support and constant reminders that I need to finish what I've started;

My children, *Donissa, De-Ann* and especially *Delon*, my first and harshest critics;

Professor *Norka Blackman-Richards* who motivated me through her inspiring message, "Heads and Not Tails," to move forward with this project which I had just started when I met her and for taking time out of her hectic schedule to read my first draft and encourage me, that while it required some work, it is truly something that is needed in our society;

My friend, *Racquel* who spent tedious hours editing my first draft and offering valuable critique;

My writers' group, '**Evening Star**' – *Karen E. Quinones Miller, Sharai Rucker, Akanke Washington and Carla Pharaoh,* who, week after week, worked with me scrutinizing word by word, thumbing through page after page –

critiquing, restructuring correcting errors and most of all offering encouragement all the way – even when we had to work until 2:00 a.m.;

My friend, *June,* for her encouragement and support;

My friend *Rhonda,* for putting up with my endless requests and her invaluable input;

My in-laws, *Wendine & Ted,* for their support;

My sisters, *Shondel and Deon,* who were also harsh critics and who along with my brothers, *Colin and Darren,* were ready to research any information I needed;

And of course, *Dorothy*, who kept encouraging me to go back to school. This booklet is possible because I eventually took her advice and went back to school.

Most of all

This booklet is dedicated to my brother

Linden F. Lord, MD, FACOG

After suffering a gunshot wound to the head, Linden is lying incoherent in a hospital bed in Jamaica. Proceeds from the sale of this booklet will assist in supplementing his medical and rehabilitation expense in the United States.

We pray for the restoration of his health.

For

My Parents

James & Doreen Lord

My Brothers

Rawle and James Jr.,

My Nieces, Nephews & In-laws

About The Author

Fiona Harewood always wanted to be a writer, but never really thought it possible until she started working as a part-time housekeeper for Karen E. Quinones Miller, bestselling author of "<u>Satin Doll</u>", and other novels. One day while washing dishes, she told Miller of her dream. "Put together what you have, and I'll critique it and let you know," Miller told her.

That was all Harewood needed to hear. She joined Miller's writers' group, Evening Star, in April 2002.

Prior to embarking on her dream career, Harewood was educated in Guyana, South America, where she grew up. Before migrating to the United States in February 2001, she lived in Barbados, West Indies for thirteen years and worked in the airline industry.

Harewood has since finished a Bachelor of Science degree in Paralegal Studies and will soon complete her Master's in Public Policy at Drexel University.

After completing her bachelor's program, Harewood decided to encourage people who have dropped out of school to return to academia so they, too, could also achieve the personal satisfaction that a full education can bring. This triggered the writing of her booklet – "I Did It. . You Can, Too!" Her hope is that her readers will consider returning to academia after completing this booklet and build a better future for themselves, their family and their community as a whole.

Harewood lives in Philadelphia and works as a Senior Case Technician with the Federal Government. Harewood is currently plotting her third book.

Table of Contents

CHAPTER 1:
THE JOURNEY................................... 1

CHAPTER 2:
HOW DO YOU DECIDE IF YOU SHOULD GO BACK TO SCHOOL – AND WHY? 15
- *Are you doing it for you?* 16
- *Would you like to secure a better job?* 17
- *Would you like to maximize benefits?* 20
- *Would you like to set an example?* 21
- *How should you choose a career?* 22
- *Where should you go?* 23

CHAPTER 3:
WHAT ARE THE OBSTACLES IN YOUR WAY? 27
- *Money?* 27
- *Time?* 28
- *Support?* 29
- *A Lack of confidence?* 30
- *Sacrifice?* 30

CHAPTER 4:
THINGS TO TAKE CARE OF PRIOR TO STARTING SCHOOL.. 33
- *Communicate with family members* 33
- *Child care arrangements* 34

*Communicate plans with employers
according to the environment*............... 35

CHAPTER 5:
NECESSARY RESOURCES 39
Faith 39
Find a mentor 42
Study time 45
Discipline yourself for online courses................... 47

CHAPTER 6:
HOW TO HAVE A SUCCESSFUL JOURNEY… 51
Now is your chance to start again 51
Consult with your advisor.................................... 52
Be Careful when dropping/adding courses........... 54
Attend every class 57
*Participate in class – never be ashamed
to ask questions*…………………………… 59
Complete every assignment on time 60
Start final papers/projects as soon as possible 61
Take advantage of tutoring sessions 62
Do available extra credit 63
Join study groups.. 64
Keep record of all class scores received............... 66
Stay away from plagiarism 68
Persevere with even the tough courses 69
Don't just try to pass – aim for the stars............... 70
*Keep at it – don't stop until you've
crossed the finish line* 72
"Walk" at your graduation ceremony 73

"Wisdom is a shelter as money is a shelter, but the advantage of knowledge is this: wisdom preserves the life of its possessor."

- Ecclesiastes 7:12 (NIV)

1.

The Journey

"Experience is a good school, but the fees are high." -Heinrich Heine
– Nineteenth Century German poet

So, you dropped out of school. Have you reached your full potential - all you're capable of? Do you feel satisfied – is this a decision you can live with for the rest of your life? If you have answered yes to even one of these questions, then this booklet is not for you.

In his *National Address to America's School Children* on September 8, 2009, U. S. President, Barack Obama, stressed to students:

> *And no matter what you want to do with your life, I guarantee that you'll need an education to do it. You want to be a doctor, or a teacher, or a police officer? You want to be a nurse or an architect, a lawyer or a member of our military? You're going to need a good education for every single one of those careers.*

You cannot drop out of school and just drop into a good job. You've got to train for it, and work for it, and learn for it...

Many people who dropped out of school would like to return but either don't know how, or cannot find the courage or means to do so. Well- meaning family members and friends urge dropouts to go back to school – and that's good, however, have they stopped to consider how challenging returning to the classroom might be? For some people, school is a distant memory – something they did ten, twenty or more years ago. My hope is that this booklet will encourage all dropouts -- whether from high school, technical school or college – to finish their education. Yes, going back to school will be a challenge, but I assure you, the payoff is worth it.

Fortunately, there were two individuals, at two different intervals in my life, who shepherded me back to school when I dropped out prematurely. I am glad they did this, so it is my hope, this booklet will do the same for you. Let me start by telling you my story.

I am originally from Georgetown, Guyana in South America. I migrated to Barbados, West Indies in 1988 and came to the United States in 2001. Even though I was an average student in elementary and high school, I didn't do well on exams. At age sixteen I took the Caribbean Examination Council (CXC), in Guyana, an examination taken at the completion of high school. I was examined in four subjects, English language, history, English literature, and mathematics -- and I thought I was prepared because I had really studied for the exams. But even before the results came in, I knew I did miserably. I received the equivalent of a 'C' in English literature, but I failed the other three subjects. The results disturbed me, and left me disappointed and embarrassed. It was humiliating when friends and family asked about my scores. It wasn't easy telling people, especially those who knew my head was always buried in a book, that I only passed one subject.

My parents didn't give up on me because they knew I studied hard, so one year later, they paid for me to re-take the three subjects I previously failed, and added another subject – economics - to the list, making it again a total of four. Taking the test again was quite expensive. It was difficult for my father to come up with the exam fees because he was the only breadwinner in the household, so I studied even harder than the first time before taking the exams. However, this time around I did worse than the previous year - I received no passing grades for any of the four subjects. I was distraught. That was it! I was done with school. I stayed home for over a year helping my mother with the household chores and the care of my younger siblings. Then one day my grandmother confronted me.

"Child, what's with you and being home all the time? I think you should go and do some typing or something. These days both men and women working. You cannot wait for a man to marry you and make you a housewife. Is better to work for your own money, that way, nobody can make you a fool," she said.

Maybe my grandmother had forgotten that I had failed the exams twice, so I decided to remind her.

"Grandma, you remember I tried twice and got no passing grade?"

"So what?" she screamed. "Then you will keep trying. Put on your clothes and le' me take you to the commercial school down the road."

It was no use arguing with Grandma Stella - the next day I was back in school and taking advanced English, typewriting and shorthand. The third time, as they say, was the charm and fourteen months later, I graduated with honors. With my diploma I was able to secure my first secretarial position at The Law Firm of Ashmead Chambers. I loved it. My involvement with both civil and criminal law allowed me to come into contact with people of diverse backgrounds who had both fascinating and heart wrenching stories to share.

Later, I completed a two year certificate program in secretarial science at the Government Technical Institute. My grandmother was instrumental in getting me back on the road to achievement; likewise, there is someone who is probably standing by, ready to do the same for you . . . if you let them. But even if you are without a positive driving force in your life, you can still move ahead. You can be the voice inspiring and challenging yourself to higher achievement. It bears noting that my success the third time around came while I was a teenager with no children, job or any such "adult" responsibilities. It is usually easier then. But we are talking about returning to school after being away from the classroom for over ten or more years – and once again I have a story to share.

I was 44-years-old – with three children – when I considered going back to school. It was because of a friend named Dorothy who had just completed her Masters in Adult Health Nurse Practitioner and was preparing to start her PhD. Any opportunity she got she encouraged church members to go back to school. Sometime during the autumn of 2005 I became a captive audience riding home with her in her silver-grey Honda Civic.

"Fiona, I know you keep telling me you are not thinking about going back to school, but I really believe you should," Dorothy said. I turned and looked across at her expressionless profile, her eyes fixed firmly on the traffic in front of her.

"Dorothy, why would I go stressing myself with school at this age? Not me! It's not like I don't have a job. And I know you always say I can make more money, but I don't want to be studying at this time of my life. I love it when I can go home from a hard day's work, throw myself across my bed, flip through the channels of my TV, and laugh loudly at one comedy show after another."

"Fiona, I'm telling you, it's the best thing you could ever do for yourself," Dorothy insisted. "Go back to school. If you want me to, I can help you. Just tell me what you like doing, and I will do the research, fill out the forms and do everything for you."

She slowed the car, stopping in front of my home. I got out, looked her squarely in the eyes and smiled, "Stop trying, girl, because I won't do it. Not at this age. But thanks for the ride."

I don't know why, but for days following the drive with Dorothy, her words kept preying on my mind; and every time the thoughts surfaced, I toyed with them for a little while before dismissing them. By then, I was a secretary for 26 years and I knew I wasn't happy with my career. But frankly, I felt going back to school was too much.

Four years after migrating to the United States, I was temporarily assigned to one of the largest law firms in the northeastern part of the country, as a data entry operator. When the temporary project ended after about nine months, I was the only one of five short-term employees who was made permanent. My supervisor, Barbara, said she admired my work ethics - I was always there on time, stayed late when the need arose, paid attention to detail and produced accurate work. Then the time came when my boss's superiors shortened the deadline for the project. Barbara summoned me to her office.

"Fiona, I have orders from our partners to have this project completed within the next two months, making it three months ahead of schedule. Would you lead the team and try to get this done for us?"

"I will certainly try, Barbara," I responded.

After verifying some details, my team and I went to work, even though some voiced their concern, realizing the shorter deadline meant being out of our jobs sooner than we expected. My tasks included scheduling the assignments, tracking the jobs, liaising with staff to ensure proper work flow and working many long hours inputting data into the computer. The project was eventually completed two weeks prior to the newly requested schedule. My supervisor was impressed that although it meant being out of a job sooner than anticipated, I made sure the project was completed before the company's deadline. So, they hired me as a case assistant but I wanted to be a paralegal.

A case assistant is the proverbial bottom of the legal ladder. Even though I was happy to have a secure position, I knew I didn't want to stay at the bottom rung. Also, compensation at this level was inadequate to cover my family's needs. I was working with paralegals who assisted attorneys by preparing legal documents, conducting legal research and performing other complicated legal tasks. I wanted to do what they did. I read and then re-read my job description. Dorothy's words came forcibly back to me. There was no other answer - I had to go back to school.

I still wrestled with the idea - *Back to school at 44? No way, not now, it is just not possible!*

Eventually, I realized that going back to school was no longer an option – it was a necessity.

It was scary to even think about; but then I realized that going back to school was something I would benefit from personally, so the sooner I started, the quicker I would finish – after all, I was 44, not 18 years old. Fear overwhelmed me. Questions and doubts clouded my mind.

What would it feel like being the oldest person in a classroom? Would the young people make fun of me? How would I juggle full-time work and go to school, since I could not afford to quit my job?

Overall, it was a challenging experience but rewarding every step of the way. There were classes I enjoyed but there were some I took simply because they were required. I enjoyed my legal classes more than any other and I attribute this love to my passion for the legal field. Classes that involved writing legal memorandum in answer to legal issues made me come alive, especially the aspect of researching case law and statutes. American history and literature were also favorites, because topics such as slavery and how America gained its independence were always of interest to me. My love for reading and writing made me cling to literature. Math on the other hand was a problem - the figures made me sleepy. And anything dealing with science ceased to hold my attention for any period of time. Though I learned a great deal from my science, mathematics and computer classes, I believe the only reason I stayed awake during some of those courses was because they cost me a lot of money; still, I was determined to excel in them just as I did in other classes.

I recall being enrolled in only two courses during my first session – Legal Writing I and Introduction to Paralegal Studies. I wanted to take three courses, but the director of the program advised against it, since I was working full time. Before the session was half way through, I was thanking him for his guidance. Chapters in both text books were extremely long and assignments contained exhaustive writing and reading, as well as researching statutes, case laws, the Constitution and many other legal sources to arrive at answers. I remember times when I thought I found the perfect case or statute to answer my question and started drafting my memo, only to realize after wasting many hours, I did not shepardize my cases to find out whether the law was still current, or whether it had been overruled in another case. I cannot count the number of times I sat at my computer at home and literally cried because I felt I just couldn't do any more work on an assignment. However, I always felt better after those tears, because I was able to pull myself together and start again. I smiled broadly when at the end of the semester I received 'A's' for my first two courses. All of my hard work was worth it. Praise God! There were many more 'A's' to follow.

My two greatest achievements so far are graduating *magna cum laude* and receiving my Associates and Bachelor's degrees, exactly three years and six months after I went back to school. Now it is like a fire was lit in me. I didn't intend to stop there - I am taking steps to obtain a Master's degree with the goal of securing a paralegal specialist position with the federal government.

So, how did I move from thinking it was impossible for me to go back to school to being a candidate for a Master's degree? Let me share with you how it all happened - and how you can do it too!

> *"Let the wise listen and add to their learning, and let the discerning get guidance."*
>
> *– Proverbs 1:5 (NIV)*

2.

How do you decide if you should go back to school – And why?

"Learning is a treasure that will follow its owner everywhere."
- Chinese Proverb

The most important thing to remember when making a decision on whether to return to school is that you have to do it for YOU. You shouldn't go back to school to please someone else; you must do it for you. If you're not going back to school for the right reasons, you will lack the strength and conviction to see it all the way through. Of course not everyone can or has to go back to school, so how do you decide if additional schooling is for you? There are some questions you need to answer honestly to help you with your decision. Questions such as:

- Have you completed high school?
- Are you satisfied with your compensation package?
- Are you longing for a career change?

This list is by no means exhaustive, but the questions listed are pertinent. Before you take the decisive step to go back to school please consider the following:

Are You Doing it for You?

Do you feel like you have not really accomplished anything for yourself? Have you been helping everyone else and neglecting your own needs? Have your circumstances forced you to drop out of school? Are you tired of working for minimum wages that cannot even pay half of your monthly bills? Are you tired of living in poverty and being 'society's tail'? Don't be dismayed; going back to school and completing it successfully, will help you realize some of your broken dreams. If you have never done anything for you, here's your opportunity. Go back to school now. Do it for you. Do it now!

It is often said *procrastination is the thief of time* – stop putting off going back to school. Experience has taught me it is better to get up and do what needs to be done while I can, instead of putting it off indefinitely. So let me encourage those of you who need to ponder and consider a decision for a while before you take action -- just know, the longer you wait, the harder it becomes. The more you count the cost, the more unreachable the goal may appear. And the reality is that most people postpone making the decision because inside they're afraid of failing – fearing they do not have the strength to complete their task. You can take courage in Philippians 4:13 of the Bible which says – "I can do all things through Christ which strengthens me." And I am living proof of that because there were many times when I thought I couldn't make it but I persevered and in doing so, I became stronger and accomplished the goals I set out to achieve.

Would You Like to Secure a Better Job?

No one grows up thinking they will get in a dead-end job and stay there for the rest of their lives. Don't misunderstand me – starting at a low-paying job is not something anyone should disrespect. There is value in honest work and we have to start somewhere. However, you can't be satisfied staying in one place with no opportunity for advancement. Education gives us the tools to move our lives to different heights, so why not choose to go back to school?

In the past a high school diploma guaranteed a decent job, but today, trends have changed drastically and it is hardly possible for you to obtain a good job without a bachelor's degree. Further, a college degree is the most decisive factor for climbing the economic ladder and can usher in the start of a successful career. I was fortunate enough to attend an Education Day celebration where Mrs. Norka Blackman-Richards, a professor at Queen's College in New York, delivered a soul searching message, titled "Heads and Not Tails." In her stirring remarks, the professor said, "When we do not achieve academically, failure does not stop with us. We impact ourselves, our lives, our communities, the nation and our offspring."

A bachelor's degree is an excellent start. You may be stuck in a job where you are passed over every time a promotion comes around, simply because you do not have the necessary qualifications. You may even be performing at an outstanding level but your compensation does not reflect your competency merely because your qualification doesn't indicate that you hold the educational requirements that are essential for the position. Going back to school and obtaining your degree will make you more marketable and will open doors you have never dreamed possible.

The study, "Demography as Destiny, (Higher Educational Attainment Equals Greater Earnings)," states that *educational accomplishment runs parallel with earnings potential*. In 2001 the average annual earnings for high school dropouts was $20,000, the same since 1975; those with only a high school diploma earned around $25,000; employees with a bachelor's degree, their salaries increased from around $40,000 to over $50,000. Further, this 2006 study found that employees with graduate or professional degrees had their salaries increased to nearly
$75,000. Do not sabotage your financial potential, go back to school. Make it your goal to do everything you can to increase your earning power.

Would You Like to Maximize Benefits?

The cost of medical insurance in the United States is extremely high. If you do not have a job that offers medical insurance it is almost impossible to afford this coverage. Most high school dropouts are unable to afford medical insurance for themselves and family. Not only do you get good medical coverage when you are qualified for a job, but you also have the opportunity to command an excellent benefit package, including pensions or other retirement options, tuition reimbursement for yourself and family members, paid vacation and sometimes stock options.

I recall while I was working as a part-time house cleaner in 2002, I had some medical issues and collapsed one day at church. I was taken to Albert Einstein Medical Center, held for two hours and then sent home. The bill for those two hours was close to $4,000.00. I had no medical insurance. Additionally, I was referred for a CAT scan which cost approximately $6,000 dollars. It is stressful to have huge medical bills without knowing how they will be paid. Going back to school and obtaining a better job with benefits will provide medical insurance for you and your family.

Would You Like to Set an Example?

You have heard it said many times over, "I want to be like Mommy or Daddy." What does your child see when he or she looks at you? You have an opportunity to set a great example not only for your children, but also for your peers. The choices you make today may influence generations to come. Imagine being the first in the chain to break the cycle of poverty, of barely making it, no longer living from paycheck to paycheck.

It helps your children tremendously to see their parents being productive rather than relying on government aid to survive. It is now within your reach – just go back to school and take that first step.

Many people waste time doing things like partying and watching television instead of using their time more effectively. Is this what you want your child to do? Too many of us live in regret, thinking of what we could have done differently. I have heard and it has been my experience - decisions made before you are twenty years old, often impact your life way into middle age or later. Why waste valuable time now to regret it later? Why postpone what can be done now? Why not take the advice and opportunity being offered by our President and so many others?

My son started college about six months after I did. He graduated Valedictorian from junior high and proceeded to one of the leading high schools in Philadelphia. After he started college, he didn't focus on maintaining straight 'A's', and by his second year studying was no longer a priority. At completion of my courses I started sharing my grades with him and he saw how determined I was to obtain an 'A' in every class.

Eventually, he decided if Mom can do it, then so could he. His grades got better and have remainedthatwaysince.

How Should You Choose a Career?

Is there something that you like to do and whenever you think about it you get excited? Do you have dreams of becoming an engineer, a chef or a nurse? Then choose what you love and admire, as a career. There is nothing worse than following a path for which you have no enthusiasm. I believe one of the reasons I did well when I went back to school was because I chose legal studies – the field I am passionate about. If you choose something you have a genuine interest in, you will be more motivated to complete it and learning will be easier.

Where Should You Go?

Start at the institution that fits your place in life best. If you are unable to pay for an expensive private institution, or their admission requirements are too stringent, maybe community college might serve you better. After all, you can transfer if or when your situation changes. Remember, school is challenging enough, don't borrow other issues that can be avoided.

The first thing you need to do is to ensure that the college you are about to choose is accredited. It would be a terrible waste of time and resources to find out "after" completing your program, the diploma or degree you have is unacceptable. Let's talk a little about accreditations.

According to the United States Department of Education, for the most part, colleges and universities operate independently. The government does not have a body exercising sole nationwide control over educational institutions. Therefore, these learning establishments vary widely in the character and quality of their programs. The practice of accreditation came about to enable evaluations of these educational facilities, ensuring that they operate at the acceptable level of excellence. You should check the list provided by the *U.S. Department of Education at* http://www2.ed.gov/admins/finaid/accred/index.html to ensure your potential college is accredited.

It is also wise to consider location. The college I attended was located within walking distance from my job. Making a long commute to school puts you at a disadvantage; you don't want to get there too tired to be able to focus in class.

Location isn't the only factor that you need to consider when deciding what school to attend. I had a choice of going to school at the community college in my area or a private college. The community college was closer and less expensive, but these two factors also led to a longer and more tedious application process, due to the sheer volume of applicants. It was almost impossible to speak to someone on the telephone and nothing was resolved without joining long lines. For these reasons I opted for a private college and during my lunch break I completed my registration. Using time wisely is essential.

> *"I urge you, ... to watch out for those who cause divisions and put obstacles in your way that are contrary to the teaching you have learned. Keep away from them."*
>
> *– Romans 16:17(NIV)*

3.

What are the obstacles in your way?

*"Paralyze resistance with persistence." -Woody Hayes,
American football player and coach.*

I wouldn't suggest the decision to return to school is a simple one. After all, it is said, *nothing good comes easy*. For a parent, going back to school requires sacrifice. Many cannot afford to quit their jobs to focus on school. This chapter will provide tips on how to balance school with the duties of a working mother or father. Let's look at some of the obstacles you might encounter on this journey:

Money

Can you afford it? The answer is, yes you can - there is financial aid offered for many technical courses and maybe all associates, bachelors and masters' degrees. And even if you are among those who do not qualify for financial aid, the federal government assists with grants and loans, work study and other such opportunities. The key is to research - the internet has a world of information that can get you started - http://www.fafsa.ed.gov is the best place to start your search to find funds for school. For those of you who don't have access to the internet, your public library offers this service, as well as a wealth of information regarding funding. Additionally, there are many non-governmental organizations that grant scholarships. You can find information on scholarships and fellowships on the internet via "Google," "Ask" or other search engines. Many colleges and universities also offer these aids.

Time to Attend and Finding Time to Study

It may be better to start with evening courses according to your work schedule. If you work at nights, then you may consider part time, day classes, because it will be tedious to work and go to school full time. In order to do well in school, you will have to dedicate some time to studying and completing assignments.

While studying for my Bachelors in Paralegal Studies, I worked from 8:00 a.m. to

4:30 p.m. and I studied during the early hours of the morning before I started preparing for work. I would get up around 4:00 a.m. and I found these hours most peaceful. I was well rested and there was complete silence to help me concentrate on the task at hand. Subject areas that were challenging were also better to tackle after resting. Now, choosing a time in no way suggests this is hard and fast. There were many nights when my head was buried in a book, or my eyes focused on the computer screen, from the time I got home from work around 6:00 p.m., until the early hours of the following morning. Yes, it can get hectic, but remember, it will not be like this always, and it pays off in the end.

Support

Remember, everybody will not applaud your efforts, so do not expect good wishes and encouragement from everyone. Not having the right support can be discouraging but remember, you are doing this for you and it will bring you great rewards in the end.

A Lack of Confidence

You will need to stay focused and feed yourself with strength and courage, constantly. Be positive and surround yourself with positive people. Tell yourself you *know* you can do it and just do it.

Sacrifice

Some people put off going back to school because they feel the social cost is too high. Many aren't prepared to give up their life styles and are unwilling to sacrifice anything. If you are one of those nightly or weekly party goers, you may have to forego most of these social activities, but there will be opportunities, limited though they may be, to have some fun. Actually, taking a break every now and again is a good way to release stress after hectic assignments, or exams and it gives you the strength to refocus on the task at hand. But don't use this as an excuse to go overboard.

While I was in school, friends and family quickly learned if they invited me to a function which would last several hours, I would bring at least one text book. In that way, whenever there was a lull in the festivities I could use the downtime to catch up on my studies.

> *". . . But one thing I do:*
> *Forgetting what is behind and straining toward what is ahead, I press on toward the goal to win the prize . . ."*
>
> *– Philippians 3:13-14(NIV)*

4.

Things to Take Care of Prior to Starting School

"Arriving at one goal is the starting point to another."
John Dewey – American philosopher, psychologist and educational reformer.

Communicate with Family Members

For those of you with spouses or partners, you know your decisions impact them. Most of us are confident our families want to see us succeed and would be willing to lend any support necessary, but the reality is, four years is a long time to be patient about any situation. In the case of a spouse, there may be some role reversals as well as other challenges, so talking it out ahead of time can prevent future disharmony. Along with Dorothy, my husband also encouraged me to return to school, but I'm sure many times he questioned the soundness of the decision. After all, no one knows ahead of time, the true weight of the sacrifices returning to school requires. There were many occasions when I heard him muttering to himself that he has lost his wife to her studies. The different changes in the family dynamics should be discussed at length before returning to school. The decision made should be one that benefits all – remembering the ultimate goal is a better future for the entire family.

Childcare Arrangement

Going back to school should never be at a cost to our children's well-being, but the other spouse should not be the only one expected to meet the needs of the kids all the time. There are going to be instances when both you and your spouse may have schedule conflicts and there should always be responsible care to ensure your children's security. Even if you have school-aged children, they will need help with homework and other projects. Helping them to succeed while they are young, will prevent them from going through the difficult task of juggling school, family and work at a later age.

Communicate Plans with Employers According to the Environment

Not all employers value their human resources equally. Accordingly, the decision to let your employer know of your study plan should be based on the environment – does your work atmosphere support personal development in education? In some instances, you will find by letting your employers know ahead of time what you are doing, can help you later. This becomes helpful when you need time off or other flexibility in your work schedule, to be able to manage your school requirements. Remember, though, to do whatever is possible to keep school work from invading your employer's time.

I remember being overwhelmed with three classes during one semester and on many occasions falling behind on assignments and final papers. When I realized I couldn't make assignment deadlines and keep my usual work schedule, I spoke with my supervisor and she agreed to give me a flexible schedule. If you can plan ahead, then you may get approval for coming in later or earlier, or even using personal time. The idea is to keep employers informed so they don't think the job is no longer important to you. It is also a good idea to schedule vacation time around exams, final paper deadlines and complex assignments. In this way, you will be free from the stress of work and be able to focus on school. There will be times when you have to forego vacations. Graduating will be the payment.

> *"Make it your ambition to lead a quiet life,........and to work with your hands, just as we told you, so that your daily life may win the respect of outsiders and so that you will not be dependent on anybody."*
>
> *– I Thessalonians 4:11-12(NIV)*

Fiona Harewood

5.

Necessary Resources

"Faith is like radar that sees through the fog - the reality of things at a distance that the human eye cannot see." - Corrie ten Boom, A Dutch Christian Holocaust survivor.

Faith

I mentioned earlier, faith is what I leaned on to get me through the difficult phases of returning to school. I realize there are skeptics, but I know faith works for me. Remember I said questions and doubts plagued me about returning to school? Well they also followed me there when I started, so I allowed my faith in God to quiet me before the start of every class. I focused on the end of the semester and believed in the possibility of earning an 'A'. Everything else in between was just the process I had to endure. No matter what your belief, rely on it and your personal strength to see you through.

There will be challenging courses. There will be subject matters you love to learn about and then there will be others that will make you question if your brain is wired like other people's – you simply won't get it, at least not immediately. As I mentioned before, math was my most difficult subject. Here again, I prayed when it got rough, but the Bible says, *Faith without works is dead,* so I had to find help, too.

Whenever I had a difficult course, I sought the help of a few friends and my children - even my daughter who was then in high school, assisted me. Many times I left the classroom confused, but I vowed not to return in the same state of mind. I utilized tutors, did as many practice problems as possible, asked questions in class – I explored all possibilities so I could understand and pass. I was determined not to just get by in challenging courses, but to comprehend the subject matter and pass them with honors. Why have I said all of this? Because I need you to understand it is okay to ask for help and to learn to use the resources available to you. You may say you don't have the support, but if you are willing to ask for help you may be surprised. It was my experience that friends I reached out to and asked for assistance while I was in school, helped me along - they took time out of their busy schedules to help me work through my academic struggles.

Getting assistance with assignments is one thing – but during the mid-terms and finals, you will be on your own. The trick is to prepare beforehand. My strategy was to rework homework assignments with which I struggled and received assistance. I would go through each step several times until I felt confident I understood everything. There was no point in getting an 'A' in a homework assignment I was helped with if I still didn't grasp the concepts.

Remember, the tests scores will let the teacher know if you understand the material or not because there will be no one helping you as you take the tests. My personal success story? I passed every math course with an 'A.' So don't ever give up - rely on faith and persevere. If I were able to move from a failing grade to a grade 'A,' you can definitely do so, too!

Find a Mentor

You may ask, "What is a mentor and why do I need one?" Well, a mentor will have confidence in you and assist you in achieving your goals. He or she will be concerned about you, listen to you and be your friend. Mentors will be advantageous to you because they can guide you through a problem you may be facing, help you focus on your goals, assist you with preparing for college, aid you in meeting interesting and successful people, offer support with test preparation, be a source of encouragement to you so you can realize your dreams and be an asset in many other areas of your life. You may even later decide to mentor someone.

A mentor can be your teacher, your guide, your motivator, your counselor and should also be someone you respect and admire. Possible mentors can range from a parent, to your next door neighbor, to a class mate you admire, or a successful person in the field in which you are interested. Although I never had a personal mentor, many people whom I came into contact with were instrumental in helping me progress. The saying *"There is nothing new under the sun"* suggests someone else has passed that way and you can learn from their experience... for example, during my second semester, I was at a gathering where a young lady was singled out and congratulated for graduating *summa cum laude*. I didn't even know what it meant to graduate with such an honor, so at the end of the event I found Andrea, the young lady who was acknowledged for her outstanding accomplishment, and inquired about her achievement. I learned that *summa cum laude* is Latin for 'with greatest honor.' It is followed by *magna cum laude* (with great honor), then *cum laude* (with honor). The guidelines for achieving these honors vary across universities. When I asked Andrea how she managed to obtain a GPA high enough to garner such an honor, she told me she shunned everything that was a distraction during school, studied hard and rested well at nights because she found when she did not have enough sleep that it was difficult for her to concentrate in class. I decided then, the *summa cum laude* honor was certainly something I should aim for. A few years after this conversation, although I did not make the highest honor, I graduated *manga cum laude*.

Now you may ask, "How do I find a mentor?" Start by identifying what you need. In your case, you may need someone to guide you along the path of returning to school or someone to help you with a difficult assignment. Then construct a list of all the people you know and include parents, friends, neighbors, pastors, coaches and many others. Remember, these should be successful people you love, admire and respect. Be sure not to limit your list to a certain age group or gender, because you never know where your help will come from. Also, add to your list people whom you think will help you to find a mentor.

After your list has been completed, you should contact these people. In contacting each person you should ask him or her, the question that is foremost on your mind. In this case it may be, "I am returning to school, I need someone to help me along, can you help me?" If you have already gone back to school, you may need someone's help with an assignment. In that regard, pointedly ask, "Can you assist me with a math assignment?" If you find that the person seems uninterested or has no knowledge of how to assist you, then you might ask him or her to recommend someone who can help you. If he or she doesn't know anyone who can help, or refers someone with whom you are not comfortable, proceed to the next person on your list.

Study Time

I have always admired my younger brother who is now a gynecologist. While he was in grade school he scarcely studied and never paid too much attention in class -- judging from the many complaints my mom received regarding his disruptive classroom behavior. I used to wonder how it was possible for him to always get straight A's in school! Later, though, as he approached the age where he had to take the Caribbean Examination Council and his university exams, his attitude towards studying changed, and his head was always buried in a book. That's when I realized, no matter whom you are, you cannot make it if you do not study. That being said, it is essential to study to maintain good grades. Personally, I found it's easiest to study while what I did in class was still fresh on my mind, rather than waiting until days later to crack open the books. But you will develop your own study habits. The essential thing is to set aside time to study.

If you have kids finding study time can be challenging but don't be dismayed, it can work! If you have to study while the children are up, ensure they are fed and their little needs are taken care of. For those capable of reading, give them interesting books and encourage them to do like mommy or daddy is doing. Remember, just as children learn the negative things they see, they also learn the positive. If they attend school and have homework, if you can manage it, do yours while they do theirs. If you cannot accomplish both tasks, assist the children with their homework first, then make time for yours. Remember, everything good requires sacrifice.

For the younger children who are not in school and can use a coloring book, give them crayons and encourage them with "smiley stickers" for good behavior while Mom or Dad is studying. Try not to let the television parent your child while you do school work. It has been proven that too much television exposure has negative effects on children. If you have to sit your child before the television, find an educational show or DVD that they will like that is both entertaining and educational.

Discipline Yourself for Online Courses

With advanced technology, many colleges offer online courses and for some majors the *virtual classroom* is required. Some students prefer online courses because they do not have to sit for hours in a traditional classroom. Others, like me, are not sold on the online classroom -- I believe the workload is often heavier than traditional classes. When choosing online courses, make sure you have good time management skills because these courses have heavy workloads and strict deadlines.

On the other hand, online courses can be advantageous for the busy professional, the student who already spends too much time on campus and the distance learner who may be based in another city, state or country. And online courses are certainly beneficial for the winter months when travelling is hazardous.

The online course format is more stringent on the deadline for submissions; if you do not complete the required tasks at the set time, some courses lock you out of that assignment, or if there is a submission deadline, the system registers the time you submit your work, making the professor aware that your assignment is late. As such, it can be more difficult to get good grades in these courses if you lack self-control.

I Did It . . You Can, Too!

> *"Whatever you do, work at it with all your heart, as working for the Lord, not for human masters."*
>
> *– Colossians 3:23(NIV)*

6.

How to Have a Successful Journey

"Action is the foundational key to all success." –
Pablo Picasso

Now is Your Chance to Start again!

Do you feel incapable of undertaking these challenges after such a long break from school? Ask any athlete who has been injured and out of play for any length of time and they will tell you, it is normal to feel unfit when you first start playing again. Many people may be out of school for about ten years or more before starting again, so, if you feel overwhelmed, you're not alone - it is normal. Do whatever it takes to get you up to speed again - if it takes re-reading a paragraph several times before you finally understand it, then this is what you have to do. Just know it won't always be that way. I found every time I started a new course I became overwhelmed. There were times when I felt so burdened, I wanted to drop the subject or quit school altogether. This is yet another time prayer helped me to take it one challenge at a time.

Even if you didn't do well academically in high school, don't worry, you have a new opportunity to excel. Honors, such as *summa cum laude, magna cum laude* or even *cum laude*, are not for the brilliant student, but for the dedicated, hardworking student. The most important thing to remember is that you do not have to outdo anyone. Just be you and do your best.

Following are some tips that worked for me and - who knows - may work for you, too.

Consult with Your Advisor

My academic advisor played a significant role in helping me with course selection and obtaining my degree. Having spent most of my adult years in the Caribbean, when I started college I didn't know how the U.S. system worked; I was unfamiliar with words such as *credits, interim courses; add/drop period* etc. I found myself consulting with my advisor on a regular basis. It should be noted, advisors are there to assist you and if you find that you are dissatisfied with your advisor, you should contact someone who oversees the advisory staff and request a change. Working with an advisor with whom you are incompatible can create needless problems. School will be enough stress, you don't need anymore.

Since the college system in the U. S. was unfamiliar territory for me, I asked a great deal of questions. My first advisor probably became frustrated with my many inquiries; eventually she stopped returning my calls and avoided me. I felt abandoned and knew I needed to find help. At the end of each semester or session, the students are asked to fill out surveys giving suggestions or feedbacks of what could be done to make a course better, and to make college life easier. I used this opportunity to let the school know I was unhappy with my advisor's attitude and treatment. The surveys are supposed to be anonymous, but I placed my name on mine because I needed attention. I was grateful, the school without any recriminations, assigned me a new advisor. This new advisor worked with me until I achieved my degree. I am still in touch with her even now – she does her job splendidly and takes pride in helping her students. That's what an advisor should do! There were times when required courses were not offered during a particular semester, or a course was offered online only. This can be challenging since it can affect your graduation date. My advisor helped me to plan my schedule and navigate hurdles so I was able to finish the degree without delays – one of the reasons I graduated six months ahead of my four-year schedule.

Be Careful When Dropping and Adding Courses

Think twice before dropping a course – just because it is difficult in the beginning doesn't mean it won't get better. During my last year I registered for an elective course, Politics of Industrializing Nations. But even though I excelled in courses that required a lot of reading I had my doubts when I realized the class required five text books. I was already enrolled in two other classes and this was my third for the session. Worse, it fell on the last day of the week. This meant when I first entered the classroom for Politics of Industrializing Nations, I was already exhausted from the other two courses, as well as almost a week of working my job. When the professor outlined the syllabus and I assessed the requirements, I was convinced there was no way I could be successful in the elective. I subsequently dropped it and picked up economics. This was an interim course – meaning, it started three weeks into the session, which gave me some time to adjust to the other two courses. But I soon found out that this was the worst mistake I made during my three and a half years of college. I ended up getting my only 'B' on my transcript and eliminated the opportunity I had to graduate *summa cum laude*. What was more distressing, when speaking with students who'd taken the class I dropped, I learned quite a few of them received 'A's'. It is possible I would have received an 'A' also if I hadn't dropped the course because it now seems that the course was not as difficult as I originally thought. When I realized the workload of the course, I allowed frustration to get the better of me and I made an impulsive decision without first praying for guidance, as I would normally do. So remember, do not just add/drop courses on initial instincts. Think your decision through, and again rely on your faith.

Another reason you have to be careful when adding/dropping courses is that you can lose your scholarship or fellowship. Sometimes universities and colleges offer students thousands of dollars in aid towards completing their degree, but most likely there will be guidelines to receiving that aid. For example, you may have to be registered in not less than nine credits per semester or session in order to receive the financial aid. If you are only enrolled in three courses and drop one, there goes your scholarship or fellowship. Check with your school's financial aid office and plan accordingly.

Additionally, many times when you add/drop a course during the semester, the session has already started -- by this time you would have possibly missed or completed two or three classes. You should consider whether or not it is worth adding or dropping the course. If adding a course, you must be sure that you will be able to catch up with the already completed workload. The add/drop period for most colleges is about three weeks but after completing almost three weeks of course work you might as well complete the class.

While adding/dropping, you should also consider the timeframe; if you decide to drop a course too late in the semester then you may lose the fees you've paid for the course. There are specific deadlines to add/drop, so it will serve you better to keep well-informed of those dates. Some schools will still charge a percentage of the course's cost if you drop them after a certain date. Also, you should not drop a course because of first impression. For instance, some professors enter the classroom on the first day of class and appear stern, but by the second or third session you may find that professor flexible and easy to get along with. So be sure to plan your courses and when registering for classes, consider alternative courses, just in case all doesn't go well when you make your first choices. If you need to drop/add, carefully consider your decision.

Attend Every Class

Missing classes automatically puts you at a disadvantage. Not only will you miss the lecture but if you are someone who needs the classroom to understand what's going on, then you will be lost. There will be times when you want to be anywhere but in the classroom, but you still need to go! It is worse when you don't have someone who will be nice enough to share their notes, take handouts for you and let you know of homework assignments. But even if you have a dependable classmate, you're better off being in class yourself. And those times when an unforeseen emergency makes your absence necessary, then it is better to contact the professor directly and have him/her provide you with the missed material. Also, being habitually late will cause you to miss out on valuable information.

It will be to your advantage to develop a good relationship with another student just in case you have to miss a class. In that way, you can contact your classmate and get an understanding of what took place in class.

I have also found it helpful to seek out a student who is ahead in the course of study. He or she will be able to let you know what to expect with certain courses, which professors are presumably better than others and may be able to offer much more valuable information regarding the degree. Now, remember you will need somebody to help you along, so when it is your time to give back to a new student, be sure to return the courtesy.

Participate in Class – Never be Ashamed to Ask Questions

One of the best ways to learn something is to ask a question. Sometimes students feel intimidated at the prospect of speaking out in a full classroom, but remember if you leave class without asking questions, it is likely that you will remain ignorant. It is possible that reviewing at home might bring clarity, but you shouldn't count on that. When I first started attending classes I was shy. Then I learned to focus less on those around me, especially those who appeared to know it all. If I didn't understand something, I asked a question. You will find there will be someone else who needed the answer to that same question. You should also note a percentage of your grade may come from class participation.

I have found it is easier to make contributions in class when I read ahead. Participation entails preparation, contribution and listening. To gain more from your classes you should give your opinion and listen. Taking notes and focusing on the professor and classmates who are sharing help to improve listening skills. At times while in class you may find your mind wandering. Keep your mind from wandering by listening for certain prompts from your professor during discussions or lectures. These include phrases such as: "Now, this is important . . ." "The point I'd like to make is . . ." "In summary . . ." and many others. These cues will serve to help you recognize main ideas and significant points that should be reconsidered.

Complete Every Assignment on Time

The completion of assignments plays a vital role in making up your final grade. You cannot expect an 'A' in any course if you do not submit all assignments. Since it is possible to get help with homework there is no excuse not to get it done, special effort should be made to complete every assignment. It is important to check the assignment requirements from the beginning of every course to have a clear idea of due dates and how much weight each assignment has towards your final grade. There were many of my classmates who found themselves in frenzy when they started their assignments at the last minute and found that it involved more time than they thought. Don't let this happen to you

– keep a planner if necessary and always have assignments ready on time.

Just as your Bible should be your road map to life, your syllabus should be used as your roadmap for successfully completing every subject on your journey through school. Obtaining and consulting your syllabus beforehand is a valuable way to stay informed and will save you the stress that missing deadlines bring. Checking your assignments via your syllabus at least a week prior to deadlines will also serve you well.

Start Final Papers/Projects as Soon as Possible

Final papers are the standard with almost every course, so be prepared. Fourteen weeks for a semester may seem endless. And if you are doing an accelerated course, even seven weeks may seem like a long time. Don't be fooled. That time will be over much sooner than you anticipate; especially if you mismanage time along the way. I did have my moments of procrastination, but I have found my best papers were the ones which I dedicated a few hours weekly to getting them done. There are papers which require extensive research and a great deal of preparation; you do not want to leave these until the final two or three weeks of class, which will be stressful enough, as you wrap up other assignments and prepare for final exams.

Take Advantage of Tutoring Sessions

Colleges try to provide tutors for almost every subject they offer. Even when there is no tutor for a specific course, colleges go to extraordinary lengths to help students to succeed, even if it means arranging group tutoring sessions – at least my college did.

In my second year of college I registered for environmental science – another elective which required a prior knowledge of chemistry and formulas. Almost the entire class was struggling and there was no tutor for the subject. I wrote the head of Tutoring Services on behalf of my class, explaining that we were in dire need of assistance. Her response was there weren't tutors available for that subject, but said she could arrange group sessions if the two professors who taught the subject would agree to conduct them. The professors agreed and the class voted on a convenient time.

Unfortunately, Saturdays, a day I could not attend due to my religious beliefs, was unanimously chosen. I didn't worry about it – I was glad my classmates were able to receive help. I then prayed seriously about that subject and worked extremely hard. I finished that class with 97 percent – one of my highest grades.

So if you encounter difficulties in your studies, don't hesitate to schedule tutoring sessions – whether independently or within a group, especially since this service is provided for free. You are the one requiring help, so be prepared with the material and have your questions ready, this will go a long way in making these sessions more productive. Also, tutors prefer you to tell them specifically what it is you are having problems with.

Do Available Extra Credit

Extra credit is a useful tool to help boost your GPA. So, if you decide to not just pass, but to do so with honors, then this is something you want to make use of, especially since some colleges require as much as a 3.5 GPA for acceptance to their graduate programs. You should ask professors at the beginning of the course if they will offer extra credit assignments. If the professor does not plan to assign extra credit, then you know from the inception you have to work even harder. Some students are merely content with passing a course and so they disregard opportunities for extra credit. Extra credit is also an asset if you are failing a class, so if it is available, make good use of the opportunity.

Join Study Groups

If time permits, joining organized study groups can have a huge positive impact on your college experience and your grades. A well-organized study group will offer the following advantages:

No procrastination – when you are studying alone it is easy to be distracted or to postpone what has to be done. Study groups have specific times of meeting and you have to be prepared.

Learn faster: When studying alone, you may spend lots of time trying to decipher information, while in a study group you simply ask a question and another student may be able to explain what you do not know.

Gain new perspectives: Studying alone allows you to have only your viewpoint as opposed to studying with a group where perspectives are diverse and can be shared. As a result you develop critical thinking skills.

Learn new study skills: Group study allows you to meet with other students who utilize different techniques to study. Incorporating your best methods with others will be worthwhile.

Here are some tips on how to join study groups:

- Look around your class for peers with whom you would like to study
- Be friendly and keep in contact with your classmates so that if a group is being formed, you will be asked to join.
- Find out who is forming a study group and ask to join.
- When asking to join, let the person know what strengths you can contribute to the group.

- Do not form or join a study group with your close friends
- Select neutral meeting places for group meetings.
- Be careful not to take too much food to the study group meetings – food can be distracting.

Keep Record of all Class Scores Received

Many students just make a mental note of their grades when a project/paper/assignment is returned and then set it aside. This may be fine if you received a perfect score, but if not, then you should definitely check your score against the outlined grading scale to stay aware of what your final grade may be if you keep scoring at the present level. The scale will also inform you of areas in the assignment where you need to improve. Looking over your graded paper would give you a better understanding of the professor's style, as well as what you did wrong. In addition to noting your grades, you should keep your test papers handy so you can review for future exams and use them as a reference for other papers.

In one of my technology courses, Searching and Researching the Internet, my professor followed a grading system. It helped me to see clearly what I needed to focus on when given an assignment and also showed me where to place most of my emphasis. When I received my final paper in the course, I got a 'B.' I was appalled. I immediately consulted the grading system. I learned that I received 0/30 for content. *How could that be*? The professor's note stated I plagiarized. Even though I recorded the source of my information in my list of cited works, I quoted a piece of someone's work within my paper and did not place them in quotation marks. That mistake cost me 30 points. *Ouch!* Be sure not to make the same mistake. Plagiarism is treated as a serious offence in college. I continued checking the grading system and noticed I was also penalized for the way I cited a table. That raised a *red flag* because I knew I checked and re- checked the school's policy on how to cite a table. I emailed the professor the source I used and requested that he take another look at my paper. It was found at two different locations on the college's online library, the school gave two unlike ways on citing a table. I used one way while the professor was concentrating on the other. We were able to sort it out and I was given back my points. That took my paper to an 'A' minus which wasn't bad after all, but I still hurt at losing 30 points on content.

Stay Away From Plagiarism

Colleges warn against plagiarism, which is using someone else's work and passing it off as your own. If you use someone else's work and you do not cite whose it is, or where you got it from, you have plagiarized. The introduction of the internet has made completing school assignments much easier; the information highway is always available to look up something you are unsure of or for if you need additional information. But as with many forms of technology, it can be misused by students. At college level there is zero tolerance for plagiarism. These institutions are utilizing software that scans students' papers for any instance of plagiarism. It is easy to be caught and when caught the consequences can be severe. Students have been disciplined by school boards, fined, suspended and even permanently expelled and the list can go on of the penalties suffered for plagiarizing.

The best way to avoid this pitfall is to cite, cite, cite. Your professor will let you know which method of citation he or she prefers. Some popular styles are Modern Language Association (MLA), American Psychological Association (APA), American Sociological Association (ASA) and the Chicago Manual of Style (CMS). If you have to pull something from somebody else's work, cite the source you have used. Also, it is always better to summarize the piece of work as opposed to copying verbatim, but if you have to use an exact quote for emphasis, be sure to use your quotation marks. After coming this far you wouldn't want to lose much needed points or be penalized in any other way for this issue.

Persevere With Even the Tough Courses

Nothing seemed to make sense in mathematics. My dad was a math lecturer in an adult continuing education institution and he decided to help me prepare for the entrance examination for high school in Guyana. Those were months of torture. The classroom was in the living room of our home, with a chalk board nailed to the back of our front door. My dad used all his teaching skills to explain math in its simplest form. Still, I found it incomprehensible. His patience eventually ran out and I began dreading those sessions with him. Every time he thought it was time I understood a concept and I didn't, I got whipped -- but no amount of whippings helped me to understand math. Thirty-five years later, I felt a sense of victory when I shared the news with my dad - my success in obtaining four 'A's' in several math courses while working on my first degree.

"You make me proud," he said smiling broadly and grabbing me in a hug.

So, I encourage you, never give up on the tough subjects – it took me thirty-five years, but I finally got it. You can do it too!

Don't Just Try to Pass - Aim for the Stars

You never know your true potential until you have given your best. Giving your best should be your motto when you go back to school. You don't have to make this a competition with anyone else, but always challenge yourself to get the very best grade possible in every class. When I first started pursuing an associate's degree, I planned to do my best and did try very hard. I never had honors such as *magna cum laude* on my mind. I just tried my best. I ended up with two 'B's' in my associates program. My first 'B' I earned when I took civil litigation. It was a tedious course and my professor spoke too fast for me to understand. Doing well in quizzes in that course depended on the notes I took, studying them and then applying them at exams. My highest quiz score was an 80.

My second 'B,' I obtained when I took two online courses while I was on vacation in Guyana – psychology and ethics and professional legal responsibility. I tried my best with the latter and succeeded in obtaining an 'A,' but psychology required a great deal of reading – of what I considered -- uninspiring material. The required reading was seventeen chapters - I read the first four. I merely browsed through the others. It wasn't surprising when I finished the course with a 'B'. After all, who wanted to sit and read psychology while the family was having fun in the sun? At the end of my associate's degree, I was surprised I graduated *magna cum laude*. When I moved on to the bachelor's degree I aimed for *summa cum laude*, but I fell short of it and again graduated *magna cum laude*. At my college, to graduate *summa cum laude*, a student had to have a GPA of 3.95 – 4.0. My GPA was 3.8923. Even though I did not make *summa cum* laude I graduated *magna cum laude*. You can do even better, if you try hard enough!

Keep at it – Don't Stop Until You've Crossed the Finish Line

If you are like me and end up going back to school when you are over forty and you intend to pursue a career after that degree, you know you don't have all the time in the world. When I started school, my aim was to graduate as soon as possible. To do so, I knew I had to work hard and take little or no time off. I took classes every summer when there were so many other things I could be doing. But it paid off. My determination and strict regimen helped me to complete my bachelor's degree in Paralegal Studies ahead of schedule. However, even though this worked for me, you should know your own pace, but I would encourage you not to take too many, or too long breaks between your classes. I have heard classmates discuss how difficult it often is to pick up the momentum again.

And lastly . . .

'Walk' at Your Graduation Ceremony!

This is why you have been working hard during your years of study. All the late nights, the tears, the long papers, the tedious information, and the group conflicts – all of it was for this one end – Graduation!

I planned to skip my graduation ceremony for my associates in Paralegal Studies – I wanted to wait until I had my bachelor's degree. One day I was at the Walker Center for Academic Excellence and when I gave my name to sign in to use the computer, someone remarked loudly, "I know that name."

I looked around and one of the program directors was standing there beaming at me. She then went on, "You are always on the Dean's List. Congratulations!"

I smiled and responded, "Thank you."

"You should be graduating very soon, right?" she asked, extending her hand.

I shook her hand and replied, "Not really, that's only the associates. I will attend the ceremony for my bachelors."

In no uncertain terms she let me know that I have no idea what will happen before I obtain the bachelor's degree.

"Be proud of yourself and celebrate as you go along," Ms. Wooten said. "'Walk' in the ceremony for that associates and never say it's ONLY an associates, it's a degree. You earned it and you did well."

Even though a few of my friends and family members had said basically the same thing, she said it with so much force and conviction; I just knew she was right. From that point I looked forward to my graduation ceremonies. I'm glad I did walk and I am thankful for the words of encouragement I received from the program director, family and friends. Being a part of my graduation ceremony aroused some indescribable feelings. It was an awesome accomplishment -- and moreover, it gave me the courage I needed to continue with my studies – realizing my accomplishment made me want to continue. I was glad to be doing this for my children and everyone else who needed the encouragement, but more importantly, I was doing it for me. And I did it! You can do it too!

The End

Suggested Readings:

BookRags, Inc. (2011). How to form a study group in college. Retrieved from http://www.bookrags.com/articles/38.html

Center For Teaching and Faculty Development. (u.d.) Class participation: more than just raising your hands. Retrieved from http://academic.sfsu.edu/CMS_uploads/files/7faff-355.pdf\

Demography as Destiny. (2006). How America can build a better future. Alliance for Excellent Education. Retrieved from http://www.all4ed.org/files/ demography.pdf

Desmond, N. (2010). 6 benefits of study groups. Debt-free scholar. Retrieved from http://www.debtfreescholar.com/2010/02/6-benefits-of-study-groups/

FAFSA. (2010). Federal student aid. Retrieved from http://www.fafsa.ed.gov/

Kids Health. (1995). How TV affects your child. Retrieved from http://www.bookrags. com/articles/38.html

Office of the Press Secretary. (2009). Remarks by the president in a national address to America's school children. The White House. Retrieved from http://www. Whitehouse.gov/the_press_office/ remarks-by-the-president-in-a-national-address-to-americas-schoolchildren

US Department of Education. (2011). Financial aid for postsecondary students – accreditation in the United States.

Retrieved from
http://www2.ed.gov/admins/finaid/accred/ index.html

Where smart girls go to learn. (2000). EducatingJane.com.
Retrieved from http://www. Educatingjane.com/Mentors.htm

www.ingramcontent.com/pod-product-compliance
Lightning Source LLC
Chambersburg PA
CBHW050604300426
44112CB00013B/2063